The story of a GALLEON

illustrated by

Peter Dennis

Orpheus

First published in 2012 by Orpheus Books Ltd.,
6 Church Green, Witney, Oxfordshire OX28 4AW
www.orpheusbooks.com

Created and produced by Nicholas Harris, Sarah Hartley, Katie Sexton,
Ruth Symons and Erica Williams, Orpheus Books Ltd.

Text Nicholas Harris
Illustrator Peter Dennis
Consultant Dr Lucy Blue, Lecturer, Centre for Maritime Archaeology,
University of Southampton

ISBN 978 1 905473 62 5

Printed and bound in China

Look out for the ship's carpenter, an important member of the crew. Wearing his distinctive green cap, he appears in many of the illustrations.

The Age of Piracy

In 1492, Christopher Columbus, in the service of Spain, landed in the Americas. Spain claimed much of Central and South America as its own. This area, and eventually the whole of the Caribbean Sea and its islands, became known as the Spanish Main. Over hundreds of years, vast quantities of gold and silver plundered from these conquered lands were shipped back to Spain in large treasure ships, called galleons. But the sea journey was threatened by pirates ...

It is the year 1635. In a shipyard in Spain, workmen are busy building a galleon, a large ocean-going sailing ship. In the mould-loft, carpenters use patterns from the floor to mark out shapes on pieces of timber. These pieces are then cut to size in the sawpits.

Curved timbers are joined together to make the frames or "ribs" of the ship. After that, craftsmen known as the treenail mooters fix planks of wood to the frames with wooden pins (treenails), to form the outside "shell" of the ship.

Caulkers fill and waterproof the gaps between the planks by hammering in rope fibres and coating them with hot tar, or pitch. Rope-makers twist thin strands of rope together to make thick, strong ropes, while in the forge blacksmiths make iron bolts and nails.

A year later, the galleon is in a port on the Spanish Main. The crew are loading it with treasure to take back to Spain. They use winches or pulley systems attached to the masts to haul up the heaviest chests.

Guards keep watch on the treasure while it is on the quayside. Stores of food, fresh water, beer and wine are also loaded, tightly sealed in wooden barrels. These will be the only source of food and drink for the sailors until they arrive back in Spain.

The galleon leaves port, and is in full sail on its way back to Spain. Some of the crew rest in their bunks while others are hard at work cleaning out the cannons and adjusting the sails. Below deck, the helmsman steers the ship using a whipstaff, a long lever that moves the rudder at the back of the ship.

In the galley, the cook and his assistant prepare a meal for the captain. A guard stands at the door to the treasure store. On deck, off-duty guards (Spanish soldiers) enjoy some music, while the ship's carpenter repairs a flight of steps. A noble passenger and his wife admire the view.

Only a few of the crew notice the approaching fleet of small pirate boats, but it is too late to sound the alarm.

M oments later the pirates swarm on to the ship, brandishing their weapons – pistols, muskets, cutlasses and daggers. The soldiers rush to grab their own weapons while the crew fight back with whatever comes to hand. Within moments, there is complete chaos on board ship. The nobleman, his wife and her maid look on with terror.

The pirates charge below decks in search of treasure and supplies, including weapons, food and drink. They attack the crew and guards before they have time to arm themselves.

The fighting is over, and the pirates are victorious. Many of the Spanish guards have been killed. The pirates tie up the crew, or hold them under armed guard while they empty the galleon of as much treasure as they can find. The captain and his officers are thrown overboard to the sharks. One pirate boat takes away the wealthy passengers to be held to ransom, as well as some of the crew to be used as slaves.

The pirates take treasure such as gold and silver from the galleon. They also load up their boats with food, drink, weapons and ammunition, medicines, sailcloth, ropes and even items of furniture. They sometimes take the ship itself, but this large, heavy galleon is of no use to them. They decide to sink it.

The pirates attach barrels of gunpowder to the side of the ship. When their companions are well clear of the galleon, the last few pirates will light the fuse and row away as fast as they can before the barrels blow up.

The pirates bring their haul of treasure, weapons and supplies to the shore, where they will divide them up. They celebrate their victory with a barbecue of wild pig meat. The pirate captain forces the nobleman and his wife to sign a ransom note for their safe release. As the last pirate boats reach the island, the galleon explodes.

The wrecked galleon rests on the sea bed. A gaping hole has been blasted in its side by the force of the exploding gunpowder. Water now fills the ship, causing light objects to float out of the hole. In one small storeroom lies a treasure chest that has been overlooked by the pirates. Some heavy items, such as cannons and barrels of food, fell out of the ship as it sank, and now rest on the sandy sea bed.

Most of the crew of the galleon are either dead or held captive by the pirates. But a few survivors have managed to clamber up into the crow's nest. As they sit and hope that a passing ship will come to their rescue, hungry sharks circle in the water below ...

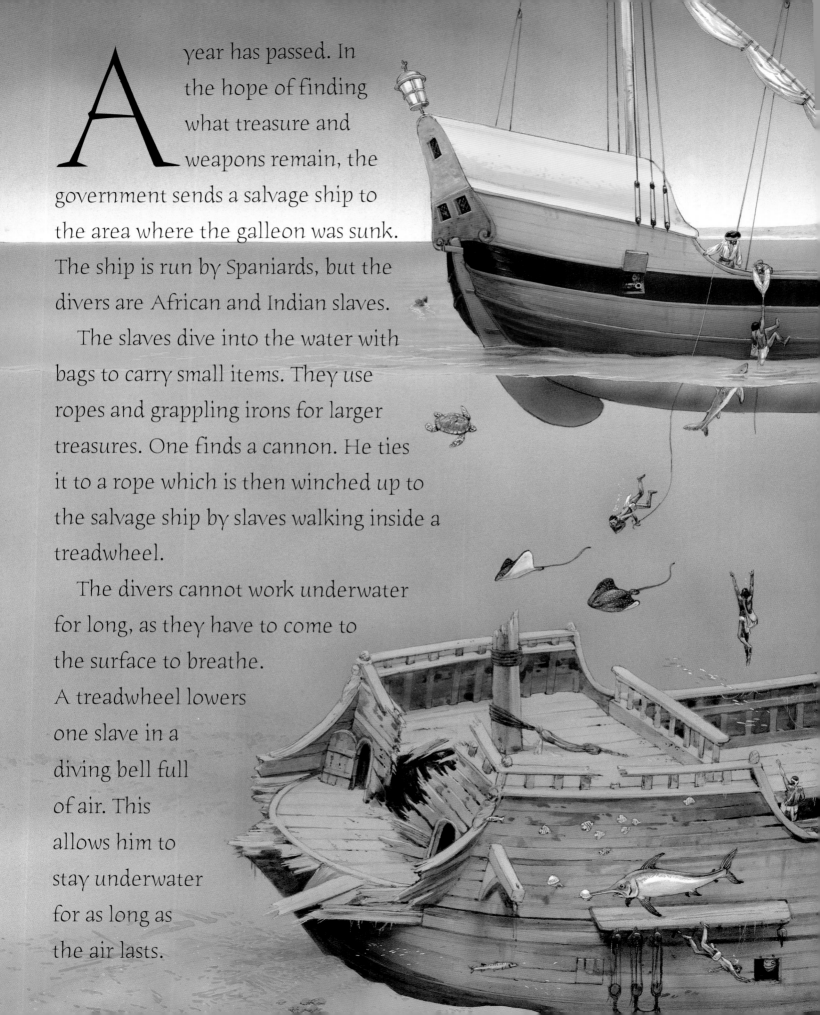

A year has passed. In the hope of finding what treasure and weapons remain, the government sends a salvage ship to the area where the galleon was sunk. The ship is run by Spaniards, but the divers are African and Indian slaves.

The slaves dive into the water with bags to carry small items. They use ropes and grappling irons for larger treasures. One finds a cannon. He ties it to a rope which is then winched up to the salvage ship by slaves walking inside a treadwheel.

The divers cannot work underwater for long, as they have to come to the surface to breathe. A treadwheel lowers one slave in a diving bell full of air. This allows him to stay underwater for as long as the air lasts.

As the years go by, the site of the shipwreck slowly becomes part of a coral reef, teeming with life. Ocean currents have covered much of the ship in a layer of sand and mud. Beneath this layer there is no oxygen, so materials such as cloth, wood or leather, which would otherwise rot away or be eaten by marine worms, are preserved. Only a few pottery jars, along with some metal objects such as a cannon, treasure chest and the ship's anchor, remain on the sea bed.

They gradually become encrusted with coral and the shells of tiny sea creatures. Rust, formed by sea water reacting with objects made of iron, has built up on the anchor and also on the treasure chest. Concretions, lumps of rust that grow bigger and bigger, have started to form.

Colourful coral reef fish swim over the buried ship, hunting for tiny creatures among the coral. Meanwhile, the wreck of the galleon sleeps on, lost and forgotten beneath the sea bed ...

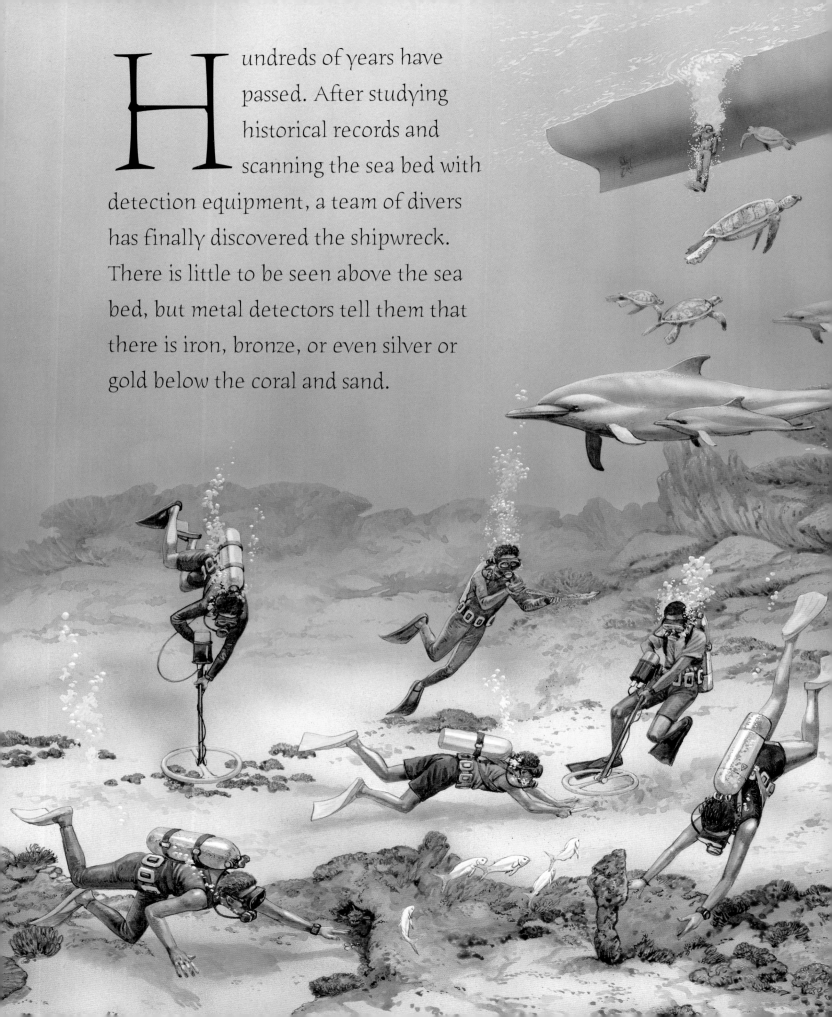

Hundreds of years have passed. After studying historical records and scanning the sea bed with detection equipment, a team of divers has finally discovered the shipwreck. There is little to be seen above the sea bed, but metal detectors tell them that there is iron, bronze, or even silver or gold below the coral and sand.

Luckily, it seems that the shipwreck has not already been discovered by treasure-hunters, and that at least some of its precious cargo remains where the ship went down hundreds of years earlier. The divers are careful not to disturb the site until they can set up a proper archaeological survey to record where they find objects.

A year later, divers are carrying out a full-scale archaeological investigation on the shipwreck site. They set up a grid of poles that divide the site into squares, to record where items are found. They clear away the thick sediment covering the wreck using suction pipes called air lifts. Old timbers, preserved for centuries below the mud, are revealed, along with pottery, cannons and even a mysterious chest.

Before moving any find, divers record its position using tape measures, label it and make sketches. They video the site, as well as taking photographs which can be put together by computers to create a map of the whole site.

Finally, the finds can be taken to the surface. Small items are placed into baskets and lifted by air-filled balloons (lifting bags), but heavy metal objects such as cannons have to be winched up from the research vessel above.

Today, a replica of the galleon is on display at a holiday resort in Spain. Although very little remained of the ship itself, from the few timbers the divers found, experts were able to piece together how the galleon once looked in its prime.

Visitors throng the ship, imagining what it must have been like to be a sailor or a pirate. Actors in costume describe life on board ship, while waxwork models of the crew portray them carrying out their daily tasks. One of them seems very familiar ...

Before they boarded, the pirates cleared the galleon's decks with musket fire. Then they lit the fuses of their fire bombs and hurled them on to the galleon's decks.

The pirates slung grappling irons over the rails and pulled the two ships together. Then, under the cover of smoke, they leapt aboard. Musketeers took aim at enemy marksmen lurking high in the rigging. Some of the men carried boarding axes which they used for smashing holes in the decks and for chopping through ropes.

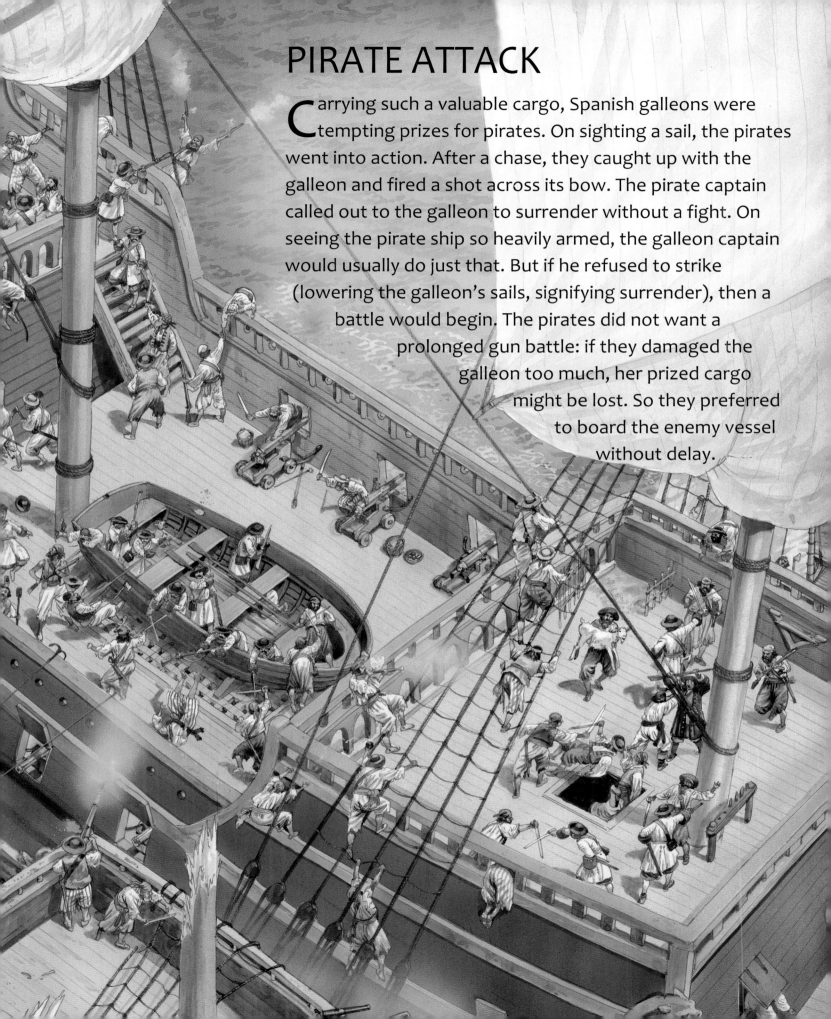

PIRATE ATTACK

Carrying such a valuable cargo, Spanish galleons were tempting prizes for pirates. On sighting a sail, the pirates went into action. After a chase, they caught up with the galleon and fired a shot across its bow. The pirate captain called out to the galleon to surrender without a fight. On seeing the pirate ship so heavily armed, the galleon captain would usually do just that. But if he refused to strike (lowering the galleon's sails, signifying surrender), then a battle would begin. The pirates did not want a prolonged gun battle: if they damaged the galleon too much, her prized cargo might be lost. So they preferred to board the enemy vessel without delay.

GLOSSARY

Archaeologist Someone who studies human life in the past, using evidence from finds buried in the ground or at sea.

Buccaneers Former hunters who turned to piracy after being driven from the island of Hispaniola by the Spanish.

Cargo The goods carried on board a ship.

Caulkers Workmen who sealed the joints between planking on a ship with greased rope fibres covered with hot tar.

Crow's nest A lookout platform around a ship's mast.

Pirate ships flew a flag known as a "Jolly Roger". Each ship boasted its own design, but many included the skull and cross swords.

Deserting Leaving a ship permanently, without permission.

Diving bell A device that allows divers to breathe air when underwater.

Helmsman The sailor who steers the ship.

Galleon A type of large sailing ship used for warfare and trading between the 15th and 18th centuries.

Galley The kitchen of a ship.

Grappling iron A hook with several prongs, attached to a rope.

Hull The main outer body of a ship.

PIRATE WEAPONRY

Pirates went into battle carrying cutlasses, daggers and axes. The cutlass's short, broad blade was ideal for use in small spaces on deck. Axes were used to chop through ropes to bring down sails. For guns, the pirates carried musketoons and flintlock pistols. Musketoons were short-barrelled rifles fired from the shoulder. Along with hand-held pistols, they were easier to use on a cramped deck.

Jolly Roger The flag flown by a pirate ship.

Musket A gun with a long barrel.

Gold bars carried on a Spanish galleon

Pieces of eight The pirate name for Spanish silver coins, worth eight reals ("royals") each.

Pirate Someone who attacks ships and steals their contents.

Privateer Someone employed by the government of one country to attack ships belonging to another.

Ransom A sum of money paid to a kidnapper for the release of the victim.

The galleon crew's daily rations included a wheat biscuit, a soup of beans, lentils and rice, and a litre of wine. Boiled salted beef and sardines might be added on alternate days. Garlic, olives and onions provided vitamins and so helped make the diet healthy.

NAVIGATION

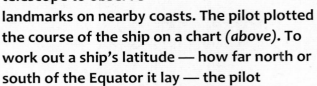

To navigate at sea, a sailor relied on a compass to tell him the direction the ship was travelling in, and a telescope to observe landmarks on nearby coasts. The pilot plotted the course of the ship on a chart (*above*). To work out a ship's latitude — how far north or south of the Equator it lay — the pilot calculated the position of the sun at noon, at its highest position in the sky, using an instrument called a backstaff (*left*). The higher it was, the closer the ship was to the Equator.

Rudder A board at the back of a ship that is moved from side to side to change the ship's direction.

Salvage Retrieving the contents of a shipwreck.

Spanish Main The coastline of Central and South America claimed by Spain after Columbus's discoveries in 1492.

Whipstaff The long lever used to steer a ship.

The Spanish treasure fleet